# Experiencing a Raw Love

## Venus Bush

BookLeaf Publishing

India | USA | UK

Presentation by *BookLeaf Publishing*

Web: www.bookleafpub.com

E-mail: info@bookleafpub.com

ISBN: 9789360947972

First edition 2024

*I would very much like the dedicate this book to everyone I have lost especially my mama Pastor Mary Adams. Who taught me how to love without measure. To My Mother Kimberley Allen I hope this makes you smile from heaven. To my two Dads... Daddy Omar Hicks and Fadja Michael Allen, I miss you both and all the life lessons you taught me. FADJA we made it.*

# ACKNOWLEDGEMENT

I would like to acknowledge my children, Elquadir, Apple, Zechariah, Isabella, and Nile, for giving me the strength to overcome challenges and pursue my dreams. Your love and support have been unwavering, and I am eternally grateful for your presence in my life. Furthermore, I would like to express my heartfelt gratitude to my best friend, Rickey A. Carter Jr., for his unwavering support and encouragement. Your belief in me has been instrumental in my personal and professional growth, and I am truly fortunate to have you as a friend.

# PREFACE

Since I was just a young child of five, I have been consumed by a burning passion for writing. It was as if words flowed through my veins, begging to be released onto the page. I always knew that I wanted to use my gift to connect with others, to speak to their hearts about life, love, and the raw truths of existence.

As the years passed, I found myself jotting down poems and thoughts in my journals, capturing the essence of my experiences and emotions. Some of these pieces were penned over a decade ago, while others were born just days before. But each one held a piece of my soul, a fragment of my being that I poured into the words on the paper.

Now, as I hold my finished book in my hands, I feel a mixture of excitement and trepidation. Will others understand the depths of feeling that went into these poems? Will they resonate with the truths that I have tried to express so fervently?

But regardless of the reception, I know that each word in this book is genuine and pure, a reflection of the different parts of my life that have shaped me into who I am today. And as I send my creation out into the world, I can only hope that it will be embraced and enjoyed by those who read it.

For it is not just a book, but a piece of my heart and soul laid bare for all to see. And I can only pray that it will inspire others to find their own voice and share their own stories, just as I have done.

# THE FEELING'S MUCH OF
# A HOT SUMMER DAY

THE FEELING'S MUCH OF A HOT
SUMMER DAY
THE FEELING'S MUCH OF A HOT
SUMMER DAY

MY BODY HOW IT BURNS FOR THIS MAN
IN EVERY WAY

HE IS INDEED A REFLECTION OF ME

A BRIGHT BEAMING LIGHT I CAN SEE

MY EYES NEVER STRAY AWAY

UNDERSTAND THAT MAN IS TO ME AS
NIGHT IS TO DAY

THE OTHER HALF I CAN ONLY PRAY

WHAT LIES AHEAD NO ONE CAN SAY

BUT THE FEELING'S MUCH OF A HOT
SUMMER DAY

I'M TASTING HIM IN EVERY WAY HIS
BUTTERPECAN CARAMEL SKIN

SO SMOOTH MMMMM ICE CREAM... I
SCREAM

ENTICING MY SOUL WHOSE MAKING ME
WHOLE

NONE BUT HE, NO NONE BUT HE

AND THE FEELING'S MUCH OF A HOT
SUMMER DAY

A ROLLER COASTER RIDING FREE

THIS EMOTION STUCK INSIDE OF ME
BURSTING OUT INTO SOCIETY

PROVING LOVE IS NOT A MYTH
UNCONDITIONAL LOVE IT STILL EXISTS!

IT DANCES ON!: A BLOCK PARTY THE
HEART BUMPIN THAT MELODY

THE FEELING'S MUCH OF A HOT
SUMMER DAY

LIKE A FIRE HYDRANT FLOWING

BIRDS STEADY CHIRPING

STREET LIGHTS A BLAZING HOT97

THESE CHILDREN PLAYIN

THE FEELINGS MUCH OF A HOT SUMMER
DAY

AND I WANT YOU SIR MORE THAN
WORDS CAN SAY

I LOVE YOU MORE AND MORE EACH
DAY

IN LOVE IS THE HEALING AND LOVE IS
THE FEELING

MY FAVORITE SEASON TO CELEBRATE

THAT IS WHY I WILL ALWAYS SAY

THE FEELINGS MUCH OF A HOT SUMMER
DAY

# TIME WITH REMEMBERANCE

As  time rewinds in my mind I remember a day
...

I remember a day ..

 I  remember a day of serenity so peaceful and
calm

a remembrance of pure  tranquility. I remind
myself of the unique simplicity...

The unique  simplicity of water running,
children laughing,

 cars not smashing/ ppl  not dying.. Elders not
crying.. As time rewinds I remember a time..

 A  time when common wasn't hood boys bangin
young men slangin..

 Our mothers  Layin... Layin with them catching
that sin....

Epiphany!.. Epiphany! We  can change this identity-

we can change to whats meant to be,

lesson  learned may never be

but in time we shall all see...

That this life like  yours is just a shell to me...

My mind wanders ..

Yes it wanders in  this century

# My Own Little Alpha Bit

I was young

heart so full & he came singing songs at my gate

~ wanna go outside in the rain ~

Flipped him off,

I was cross

Kept my distance far from soft.

Yet he pursued til I got weak

Caved in guard fell asleep.

He was my all

For him I'd crawl, I'd crawl the world from hell
and back if I could keep him.. he was my crack

see this love was so innocent, premature, raw, &
uncut.. it was so pure & once he left became
UNSURE

l met V. to get over M. Tried R. for months &
when I left them

W. came & my heart caved again

So I did the same thing.

I wanted to help him get over hood life, so in my
mind I became his wife

he tore me down, then gave me gifts.

thought it was a clue love didn't exist.

So I left his ass & moved along

Became a real wife & sung a new song

but a child I was still

So I left my husband

went back to what I knew.

took time off got with T. when I was through fell
for E.

His lies were new

Lol sounds sad but all true! Got with S. to get over a few, got another promise RING never got the marriage BOO

JUST Another baby 1+1=2

So headed back up north & found me a G. Sweet when he wants but an @hole in deed!! 2+1=3

F'd around & got sauce boss when 4th one came realized Shit was still the same

W. Came home & that's when I found.. Getting over life I was trying to do

But I started living LIFE  & got over all off YOU.

I LOVE my GOD & I LOVE my KIDS I LOVE MYSELF

& I'm done doing bids

So unless there's a

Ring, Bible, & License in tact it'll be my God & my 4
cause I'm not the Chicken Shack.
 don't be a judger that's ugly

# Soulmates

Two souls that instantly Intertwine, destined to forever cross paths in one form or another. Similarities, compatibility, & sexual chemistry become the ULTIMATE ECSTASY the moment your eyes tend to meet. Like a drug you get pulled slowly.. Drawn to each other like magnets. Separations often emotionally painful to began with... In thee end most may even wind up never being able to truly be together, but I believe a certain respect & genuine LOVE will always linger... Only deepening the bond each has for one another. In time the two shall always meet again, as repeated destined or in some cases doomed to forever cross paths in one form or another. ~This is my definition of a SOULMATE

# Ivy's Warning

Be careful what you say with that wicked tongue
sweet man
For the lies that you tell lead hearts straight to
hell
Be careful what you do with that wicked tongue
sweet man
 creep secrets that you keep may sink deep like
quick sand

She's not peachy NO not perfect
She tells the truth but is it worth it ?
no one believes her
 Is she speaking in vain??! No just that mind
wisdom keepin her sane
but those sane words sting like vamp. vervain

Be careful what you say with that wicked tongue
sweet man
For the lies that you tell lead hearts straight to
hell
Be careful what you do with that wicked tongue
sweet man
 creep secrets that you keep may sink deep like
quick sand

She hear them whisper why break what's not
broken?! What Fuck the fact that her heart has
been stolen?
 Bruise battered an beaten Guess her heart
equals tokens
 inserted into this game called mindfuck it was
working
Through out these "situations" the i love yous
well past spoken
love fluids exchanged those juices stayed goin ..
"I know your "situation" no I know what you
told me
if  I knew your situation There wouldn't be this
story!
An who has "situations"?? Those are for ppl who
end up on maury!!"
Thats the words that she screams outside of her
head
tries to put things to rest , he stay shaking her
bed
This lost lover's scorned and blood's now her
craving
she knows it's not right but her heart is still
aching..
 1 thing that's for sure, Ivy said for dam Sure
 is love for that  fuckface dont live here
ANYMORE

 So the next time you taking some woman to bed
just remember IVYS WORDS TIL THEY
BURN IN YOUR HEAD...

Be careful what you say with that wicked tongue
sweet man
For the lies that you tell lead hearts straight to
hell
Be careful what you do with that wicked tongue
sweet man
 creep secrets that you keep may sink deep like
quick sand!

# Right Now

Right now

They have a saying if it's not then when so they
say why not right now
right now
right now.
Right now is always the wrong time to say
something
I want to speak so loud
but when they hear me speak they say why did
you say it right now?
I'm equipped with no emotion no care no
subtlety
 a slight bit of empathy
 I come hard I come ready
Like a man I come without fail yet I come just
not right now.
See right now I have regrets and I never have
those because usually as I subdue to me The
Facts of Life that were due to me and I ride with
that
Lately I've been taking a sabbatical and acting
like a radical

I haven't gave a flying since I felt like I was
dying but no one cares no one sees All they see
is what I was not who I am or what I can be
The sad festivity amongst my visuality is that I
have to focus on the reality of it's really right
now.
 Right now is when I'm supposed to become
whatever it is I'm meant to become
To leave those at the Wayside who forgot to be
by my side when I need them the most and I can
talk all day about how I am what I am and who I
am and what I am but that would be just a boast
so I rather say right now I'm going to get the
work done I'm going to break down who I am
I'm going to be who I'm going to be I'm going to
succeed in what I'm going to succeed in because
if I look at everything and look back on my life I
feel Justified all things aside that I will never be
the perfect V I will never be the perfect me for
anyone else besides myself I can never achieve
any goal that I want to achieve focused on
someone else so I rather focus on me because
you see when you focus on you you really
eliminate the mindset of being oppressed unjust
and undo You Really eliminate the choice of
someone deciding not to choose you because
right now is the time that you should do so much
for yourself right now is when you focus on your
health, family, wealth, spirituality, stability,

mentality, your dreams as a whole.. if you won't do it who will and that's why I say mistakes may happen all day and people may get in your way but it's the choices you make it's the things that you say it's the way that you move all the things that you do yet at the end of the day it is the tone in your voice that says I can do the originality of yourself they said I already knew it because this time I didn't wait for later this time I chased the paper this time I chase the moment this time I created and didn't crave it I just made it happen because this time was my time it was the right time it was The Right Move it was the right feeling it was the right now and that's when I elevated. Right now

# Bubble Gum Lane

Hubba lived on Bubble Gum Lane right up the
street from Fruit Stripe Creek
just minutes away from the one that made him
week

He used to meet his buddy Red two houses
down from Chiclets place
She was a flower with heavy power because her
Juicy Cherry lasted for hours

See Chiclet rocked with Spearmint
they rocked so close could've been an Eclipse
and Hubba he was on the Lane
on Bubble Gum Lane trying to stake his claim

He walked with stride very much with pride
but Chiclet never caught his vibe
tried to break Ice Free the Dent in the
atmosphere
but her Peppermint Trident hit him like Winter
... No worries Bubblicious was thicker

She stayed up the way and never ignored him
she never strayed like Dentyne slogan she
Brightened his days

That Double action cemented their bond
she moved to the Lane and Hubba moved on.

Bubble Gum Lane was a grand old street but
without Bubblicious it was incomplete

Moral of the story is if your not staying focused
you may wind up with a person that ends up
being bogus.

stop chasing

# P.u.r.p.l.e Momma

Pleasant to the ones she knew
Unique to all I promise you
 Her Royal presence exuded excellence
Prosperity followed her God let blessings flow
Loyal to her family this Educated momma was a
hot commodity
man I miss you Kimberley

# Testing My Faith

Sometimes I feel God's testing my faith I try to
be the best person I can try to do right stay
positive in prayer then every time I turn around
the devil want to play taking my family away no
good jobs me and men who are snobs always in
debt I remember I once had nowhere to stay that
was fun laughing hard to keep from crying
testing my faith had me feeling like dying I don't
understand why I go through these things always
alone

# Preacher Do Me Right

False Preacher what's your teachings while
going to Cancun
Preaching Spirits you vested in manifesting
resurrections

False Preacher what's your teachings con
Cayman banking and booming When you're
taking from others and consuming?

Oh Preacher do me right when I offer up all my
offerings
Oh Preacher do me right when I'm laying up in
my coffin

Oh Preacher do me right since you always
Capitol tuck
Oh Preacher do me right when you asking for
hundreds of bucks

Did Momma wrong when I smelt it I knew what
was up
Told Momma I felt it  you dealt bullshit so
unexpected

A Preacher telling lies I was rude didn't give a
fuck

Momma told me wash my mouth I said watch
his actions he's not what's up
Momma told me be polite I was honest I couldn't
trust

Stole your way wasn't the way though sold the
church to self for a dollar you thought that way
was okay though?

Momma house was the Church and you opted to
be unjust your first lady a culprit I ever catch
ya'll you know it's up bitch

Bebe's kids from the get-go thank our creators
what did they think yo?

Preacher do me right but he wrong on my
Django
Gang squadded then we squatted broke day we
half retarded but Preacher do me right because
that's as you should... could've, would've did
right but you took it and did you

Deed fraud was the game? This shit was new...
Fraudulent Preachers in the Pulpit was
something I never knew

because of you Preachers are suspects
stay protected some are the Flu achoo

# A Good Christian

Twice married at the threshold but the Devil had
a strong hold
for both Men could mistreat one beat one cheat
simply put their flesh was weak
 A Good Christian so she forgave but neither one
was hers to keep
 they could not stay not due to her but because
she wanted more
love, life, and better mental health she craved
spiritual wealth
So she became a single Mom of two one Purple
one Blue
 working ninety hours a week Mary Adams was
never running the streets
got into God she got focused locked in..
remained devoted
 read that bible front to backwards she became a
Pastor A Good Christian of Gods Pasture

# Smile

Smile little lady your still alive so smile it could
be worse
 I wish you to know your worth
your beautiful inside and out
you never chase for clout
so even on your greyest day don't pout my love
just smile

# Ten Toes Down

I'm ten toes down bout all of mine I have alot
you see there's Nasir then Ah'Janai, Genesis, and
Nicholas let's not forget De'Mar
I'll blow it down about my crew my lil ones
forever
I'm ten toes down no matter what we all gone
stay together
I love my babies all my five I'm ten toes down
for life

# Hypocritical

I find it rather hypocritical the way people toss words
they brag and boast they really do the most
smoke drink and choke just the same but then

# I died last night

I dreamed I died again last night this time pulled
underwater with him.
Each time a different way different place but I
always see his face.
Sleep paralysis has become a common, I dread
the bed now days never knowing where I'm
going once my Rem is in state. I never saw me
actually die except for this last time. He pulled
me in the water my eyes wide in panic a
calmness then came over me and I just watched
it happen I died last night and woke today.
Amen

# Busy

Sighs and deep breathes
Chitter and chatter
Hugging and laughter
Moving stopping in a rush pushing through the
daily fuss
The bosses try to sing your praises but really you
just barely made it
Phone Calls, Emails, Social Media back to back
No time for silence now you stressed B/P ran up
Anxiety meds CHECK
Less time for bed but this is the norm when
you're Busy just Busy

# Mango

Moist Lips glisten with the golden glow
Ripe and ready to be devoured
Nectar so sweet right at its peak
Sticky when you touch it you got to eat it slow
Finish it to the pit though I know that tastes
good.
Don't you want a Mango?

# This is Raw Innocence

Honeydew mist on my window sill I open my
eyelids to the sight of the light
The sun shining bright through curtains that are
meant to shade my face
The smell of the green grass and sound of nature
the still of the silence working in my favor
On my mind is a lot that I can't turn off
What I could have been who I was back then
My children, Oh my babies I birthed and the
ones that couldn't make it.
My five I birthed who grew into their worth and
yet I've questioned mine for the longest time
So my mind wanders again to the sharp prick of
the thorns in the rose bush on beach street
594 was a safe place a sacred space a haven that
had been erased
The feel of the concrete ground under my feet as
I refused to put on shoes
The Grape Vines I used to swing from
Those experiences can't be redone
 Raw Innocence when you're young